Mount Rainer from Lake Washington. Seattle, Wash.

c. 1903

Greetings from Washington

by Lane Morgan

GRAPHIC ARTS CENTER PUBLISHING COMPANY, PORTLAND, OREGON

Panorama of Chehalis, Wash.

c. 1910

International Standard Book Number 0-932575-69-2
Library of Congress Catalog Number 88-80539
Copyright c MCMLXXXVIII by Graphic Arts Center Publishing Company
P.O. Box 10306, Portland, Oregon 97210 • 503/226-2402
Editor-in-Chief • Douglas A. Pfeiffer
Associate Editor • Jean Andrews
Illustrations Assistant • Alison M. Morba
Designer • Robert Reynolds
Typographer • Harrison Typesetting, Inc.
Color Separations • Trade Litho
Printer • Dynagraphics
Binder • Lincoln & Allen

Printed in the United States of America

A special debt of gratitude is owed to the deltiologists whose
extraordinary postcard collections and enduring affection for
Washington have made this book possible: Pat Kelsey, John
Cooper, Dan Kerlee, Harry Kelsey, Mike Farley, JoAnn
Hilston, Carl Kallgren, Marian and Peter Maronn.

For my parents
LANE MORGAN

CONTENTS

Circa dates refer to a ten-year time period largely determined by the printing styles of a particular era, the subject matter depicted, and other information providing clues to the date of publication.

c. 1910

100. Beautiful Puget Sound.
Inspiration Point from
Chuckanut Drive.

Foreword

BY PAT AND HARRY KELSEY

It is appropriate that the Washington State title in the *Greetings from...* series should come out in time for the Evergreen State's centennial celebration, commemorating its admission to the Union as the forty-second state in 1889. Just four years later, during the Columbian Exposition in Chicago, the first postcard in the United States was published.

It is likewise appropriate that the titles include the words "Greetings from." "Gruss aus" was the phrase that started it all. When well-to-do Americans made the fashionable Tour of the Continent in the late 1800s, they found cards with that phrase and colorful local scenes to mail home. Publishers in this country caught on, and the postcard as we know it was born.

Postcards, not only scenic views but greetings of every conceivable kind, became a national fever between 1904 and 1912, a period often referred to as the Golden Age of the postcard. Collecting postcards became a big thing, and it is thanks to these early collectors that so many of these old cards survived.

The old postcard illustrations remind us of a Washington, perhaps not in its infancy, but certainly in its adolescence. Today's collectors learn much from these old cards: how their parents, grandparents, or great-grandparents lived and worked, what they wore, how they played, where they did it, and what concerned them enough to mention it on the message side. Little escaped the postcard photographer's camera or the postcard artist's brush. Where else, other than on postcards, will you see what was on the corner of 8th and Main in 1910?

Stage Landing at Lake Crescent, near Port Angeles, Wash.

c. 1910

c. 1910

c. 1910

From Deception Pass, the view is to the Strait of Juan de Fuca, named for the sixteenth-century mariner and world-class liar who said it was the entrance to the long-sought Northwest Passage. Instead it leads to Puget Sound.

Deception Pass, Puget Sound, Washington. 2797

c. 1912

"See Washington First." The Surf on the Cliff in the San Juan Islands, Puget Sound. Photo by Webster & Stevens.

c. 1910

From Sea to Inland Sea

Europen explorers first reached the Washington coast in the sixteenth century, following rumors of a Northwest Passage across North America. Instead, they found hostile Indians and foul weather. "That night was a dreadful one," wrote John Meares of May 11, 1788, the day he sighted the Olympic Peninsula. "Such heavy gusts and squalls of wind succeeded each other that we were prevented from carrying any sail." Farther north, Indian traders offered him the severed and dried hands of murdered crewmen from a previous expedition.

Captain George Vancouver, another Englishman, made one last search for the passage four years later. Instead, he found Puget Sound. Once in the inland waters, the tone of explorers' journals changed. From storms and ambushes, descriptions give way to "a beautiful meadow covered with luxuriant herbage." The Nisqually Indians treated Vancouver's men with "all the Friendship and Hospitality we could have expected."

When settlers came, they too were drawn to the protected waters of the Puget Sound and the oyster beds of Willapa Bay. It took a later generation to appreciate the isolated Olympic Peninsula, the last great wilderness of the continental United States. Towns like Port Townsend, Port Angeles, and Port Ludlow grew up around customs stations and lumber mills, but the ocean coast was left to its first inhabitants, the Quileutes, Quinaults, and Makah. Even today it is Indian country. Most of the Pacific beaches in Washington are on reservation land, and the tribes still look to the water for their subsistence. The "splendid confusion" of

1162 Washington — Cape Disappointment Light-house.

c. 1905

DRAWING NET. PUGET SOUND FISHERMEN. WASHINGTON.

c. 1910

mountains behind them remained unexplored for nearly a hundred years. Captain Charles Barnes, who described them thus in 1890, was one of the first to climb beyond the outer slopes. Only a few homesteaders managed to carve out farms from the underbrush of the coastal valleys.

As logging technology improved and markets expanded, however, it was inevitable that attention would turn to the giants of the rain forest. A mild climate and plentiful rain—over two hundred inches a year in some spots—allowed the thin soil of the peninsula to produce giants—thousand-year-old cedar, spruce, and Douglas fir with bark a foot thick. It seemed impossible that mere men could make much of a dent in that forest, but the loggers were willing to try.

The title of a logging history of the Hoquiam area says it clearly: *They Tried to Cut it All*. By the 1930s, most of the lowland forest was gone, and a movement was growing to protect what remained. In 1937, Franklin Roosevelt visited the peninsula. After a tour of the scarred stumplands around Grays Harbor, the outraged president returned to Washington, D.C. In 1938, he signed the legislation creating Olympic National Park.

One of the planet's least altered ecosystems, the park is now the central political entity on the peninsula. It serves as a bellwether for environmental problems and a reminder of an older order. While scientists monitor its vital signs for damage from outside, hikers clamber through the Hoh Valley on their way to Mount Olympus. The remnants of the old salmon runs nose their way back upriver to spawn and die. After ten thousand winter storms, a cedar that was old when Juan de Fuca sailed falls, letting in a little sunlight for the next generation. And the ghost call of the now-extinct gray wolf, for whom the park came too late, echoes from the foothills.

A PORTION OF WATERFRONT AND HARBOR, PORT ANGELES, WASH.

c. 1909

On Hood's Canal.

Photo by Webster and Stevens.

c. 1910

Water Street, Port Townsend, Wash.

LONG DISTAN TELEPHO

c. 1910

Now lined with gift stores and ice-cream parlors, Water Street in Port Townsend was a gathering place for hard-drinking Fraser River gold miners. "Sodom and Gomorrah wasn't in it," said one veteran of its nineteenth-century heyday. Old-timers boasted that you could smell whiskey in the dirt to a depth of ten feet.

POST CARD

THIS SPACE MAY BE USED FOR CORRESPONDENCE

FOR ADDRESS ONLY.

U.S. POSTAGE
ONE CENT

Am afraid by the time
you get this reciept will
be all out of the notion for
Clam chowder but come day
& I will make you some.
first cut bacon in squares
& fry in kettle then fry potatoes
& a small onion in bacon
until nearly done pour
on some water season with
salt, pepper, & bay leaves & let
steam until done put in
chopped clams & let cook for
about five minutes then pour
in milk & a small lump of
butter.
Mrs. E. A. Brooks,

Miss Emma M. Hall

Regents Park

Tacoma

Wash.

W. J. Hill"

c. 1909

A Salmon Cannery

c. 1910

A Fish Trap on Hood's Canal,
Washington.

c. 1910

INTERIOR OF CANNING FACTORY, PUGET SOUND, WASHINGTON.

c. 1910

c. 1907

Smelt Fishing at La Push. West Coast of Washington.

3615   The Old Indian Whale Hunter of Puget Sound

c. 1905

The Makah of the Olympic Peninsula were extraordinary seamen, hunting whales from ocean-going canoes. After the kill, a crewman would dive into the Pacific and tie the animal's mouth shut so the carcass wouldn't fill with water.

3604   Indian Boat Race

c. 1905

PUGET SOUND INDIANS.

c. 1907

3619 Fisherman & Family. (Puget Sound Indian.)

c. 1910

Gilnetters Waiting turn of the Tide, Puget Sound, Wash.

c. 1910

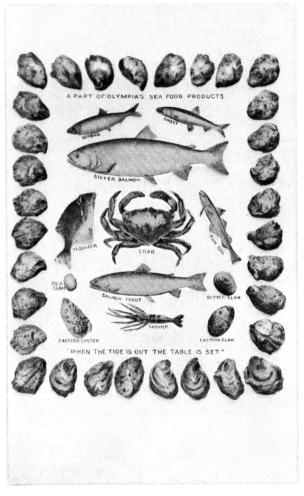

c. 1910

Seafood, and especially salmon, was the mainstay of the coastal and Puget Sound Indians. White settlers turned the resource into a business and wrote odes to "acres of clams."

c. 1907

Draining from the glaciers of Mount Olympus, where snow-fall can reach 450 inches a year, the Elwha flows into the Strait of Juan de Fuca. Until a dam blocked their passage in 1912, 100-pound Elwha salmon were not uncommon.

c. 1915

c. 1915

c. 1910

c. 1910

c. 1910

The Olympic Mountains are not particularly tall, but they are rugged, remote, and wet. The first expedition to cross the Olympics was not until 1890. Mount Meany is named for Edmund Meany, whose newspaper sponsored the trip.

Nº 1417. A Niagara of Murres,
Carroll Island.
West Coast of Washington.

c. 1907

Cape Flattery Lighthouse, Washington.

2796

c. 1910

Nº 1407. Spectacle Arches. Point of the Arches Group.
West Coast of Washington.

c. 1910

Nº 1416. The Knot & Spike.
Rocks off Cape Flattery, Washington.

c. 1910

A JOLLY TRIO. LONG BEACH, WASH.

c. 1905

Scene on Chehalis River, Hoquiam, Wash.

c. 1905

Souvenir from Nahcotta, Wash.

c. 1907

While Hoquiam was (and is) a working town, with a timber-based economy, communities on the Long Beach Peninsula soon replaced the export of oysters with the import of vacationers. Nahcotta now attracts a gourmet pilgrimage to an annual feast featuring garlic in every dish.

c. 1945

A wink and a miniskirt was enough to advertise the Hotel St. Regis once Seattle achieved respectability. Earlier entrepreneurs relied on sin, including several hundred hookers and a twenty-four-hour gambling house in 1910.

c. 1950

c. 1945

Seattle

In the race for prominence among Puget Sound cities, the race was not to the earliest—that was Olympia—nor to the first transcontinental railroad terminus—that was Tacoma—but to the best-promoted. That was Seattle.

Practically from its founding in 1852, Seattle got busy claiming popular symbols for its own glory. Foreshortened photographs brought Mount Rainier, actually a hundred miles to the southeast, to just beyond the Lake Washington shoreline. During the Gold Rush, Seattle annexed the idea of Alaska so efficiently that many Easterners still think Skagway is just up the road. Railway tycoon Jim Hill applied the same techniques to Asia.

At first the boasting was more like whistling in the dark. The first settlement on Elliott Bay was named New York-Alki. Alki means "pretty soon" in Chinook trade jargon, and the name lives on at Alki Point. In view of the collection of four dank cabins and twenty-four damp inhabitants, this may have been more a sour joke than a pledge, but the area attracted a collection of dreamers and schemers who could make surprising things happen.

After moving to better harbor across the bay, Seattleites built a sawmill and a skid road and commenced logging the hillside. They built their city around the stumps. At the first meetings of territorial government, they lobbied for the capital, lost, and settled for the right to build a euphemistically named university. The skid road served its purpose and disappeared into the language as a neighborhood of lost dreams. The overblown grade school became the mammoth University of Washington.

Seattle and Mount Rainier, from Kinnear Park.

Photo by Curtis & Miller, Seattle, Wash.

c. 1910

c. 1955

In time, Seattle, began to distinguish itself for its brashness and its luck. When the Northern Pacific chose rival Tacoma for a terminus in 1871, Seattleites got out pick, shovel, and bravado and set about building their own railway line. Other slighted cities did the same, but Seattle's effort reached the lucrative coal fields near Renton, not far but far enough.

When the business district burned in 1889, boosters saw opportunity in the ashes and rebuilt in brick. While Tacoma children were still chanting "Seattle Seattle, death rattle, death rattle," Seattle was already benefiting from an influx of skilled workers. The buildings they created are now a magnet for tourists.

When the steamer *Portland* arrived with a ton of Klondike gold in 1898, an inspired promoter named Erastus Brainerd was there, ready to persuade the world that the only reasonable route to riches went through Seattle.

Nor was Seattle content to accommodate itself to the world as it found it. Inconvenient hills were sluiced into the harbor. Lakes Washington and Union were linked, then connected by locks to the Sound. The famed Olmsted Brothers designed an elegant system of parks and boulevards and did their best to eliminate the uncouth native conifers.

By the end of the Gold Rush, Seattle had earned one of its self-bestowed compliments. It was the Queen City of the Pacific Northwest, the biggest, the boldest, and the bawdiest. Its civic leaders celebrated with plans to build a 500-bed whorehouse.

The freewheeling businessmen of that era would hardly recognize their city today. Middle-aged and middle-class, Seattle worries about its reputation and, at the same time, tries to hang on to its heritage. The Pike Street Market and Pioneer Square would look familiar to the time travelers. The ethos that preserved them from the wreckers' ball might not.

c. 1910

c. 1910

c. 1945

The Pike Place Market opened August 17, 1907, and was instantly popular. "The next time I come to this place I'm going to get police protection," one rattled farmer told a reporter after the first day of business. Swarms of shoppers had picked his cart clean in minutes.

PART OF SEATTLE FROM AN AEROPLANE.

101353

c. 1925

RESIDENCE DISTRICT, QUEEN ANNE HILL. SEATTLE U.S.A

SHOWING WEST SEATTLE AND BLAKE
AND OTHER ISLANDS

c. 1910

CANAL LOCKS, SECOND TO PANAMA, SEATTLE, WASHINGTON

c. 1950

1481 – Cedar Lake, Washington, Source of Seattle's Water Supply.

c. 1910

Beautiful Seattle. A Typical Residence Street,
The Cascade Mountains in the distance.

c. 1910

UNIVERSITY OF WASHINGTON AND SEATTLE YACHT CLUB, SEATTLE, WASHINGTON
SHOWING MT. BAKER IN DISTANCE

c. 1945

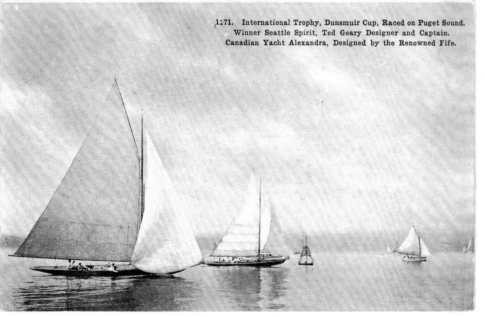

1271. International Trophy, Dunsmuir Cup, Raced on Puget Sound.
Winner Seattle Spirit, Ted Geary Designer and Captain.
Canadian Yacht Alexandra, Designed by the Renowned Fife.

c. 1910

PHOTO BY F H. NOWELL.

Yachting on Lake Union,
in The Heart of The City of Seattle.

c. 1910

1188 Steamer Vashon One of Seattle's Numerous Ferries

c. 1910

DOCK SCENE SEATTLE

c. 1910

The Seattle docks were the hub of a network of freighters, Mosquito Fleet steamers, and schooners that dominated transportation until after World War I. Sailing ships worked alongside steam well into the twentieth century.

Section of Water Front, Seattle, Wash.

c. 1910

2123—Lake Washington Floating Bridge, Seattle, Washington

c. 1950

BOAT HOUSE, LAKE WASHINGTON, SEATTLE, WASH.

c. 1910

PART OF "RIVIERA DRIVE" AROUND LAKE WASHINGTON, SEATTLE, WASHINGTON

c. 1945

By the turn of the century, a ragtag group of floating shacks lined the Duwamish Waterway, while well-to-do Seattleites moored their summer homes on Lake Washington. Said the Seattle *Post Intelligencer* in 1908: "They idle away precious hours, forgetting that the real object in life is to make money, and that time is money."

660 - CHIEF SEATTLE.

c. 1910

Indian Basket Weavers. Seattle, Wash.

Made in Germany.

c. 1905

Copyright 1906, Lowman & Hanford Co.

1141. Princess Angeline, Daughter of Chief Seattle

c. 1906

E. M. Sammis took the only studio portrait of Chief Seattle in 1864. The aging Duwamish leader wore plain clothing and kept his eyes closed. Darkroom artists added the painted designs, fringes, and glazed stare.

c. 1905

c. 1910

c. 1910

Pioneer Square marked the boundary between conventional business and the sporting life. Its centerpiece was a totem pole stolen from an Alaskan village. Today's pole, which was paid for, is a copy of the original.

THE TRIANON BALL ROOM, SEATTLE

c. 1925

THE TRIANON BALL ROOM, SEATTLE

c. 1925

CHAUNCEY WRIGHT'S RESTAURANT.
110 OCCIDENTAL AVENUE,
SEATTLE.

c. 1910

LOBBY OF PERRY HOTEL, SEATTLE, WASH.

c. 1910

Hotel Lincoln, Seattle, Washington.

c. 1910

38 - Hanging Garden, Hotel Lincoln, Seattle, Wash.

c. 1910

One of Children's Public Playgrounds, Seattle, Wash.

Photo by Pe H. Nowell.

c. 1910

c. 1910

Second Ave. from Madison St., Seattle, Wash.

c. 1910

Window Display of Children's Goods
—the finest stock of children's and
infants' wear.

THE BON MARCHÉ
COR. 2ND AVE. AND PIKE ST., SEATTLE, WASH.

c. 1910

ALASKAN CURIO SHOP, SEATTLE, WASHINGTON.
UNIQUE SHOP IN THE WORLD. ON THE COLMAN DOCK FRONT.
J. E. STANDLEY, PROP.

c. 1910

INTERIOR OF YE OLDE CURIOSITY SHOP, SEATTLE, U. S. A.
LOCATED IN THE COLMAN DOCK. MOST UNIQUE SHOP IN THE WORLD.
J. E. STANDLY, PROP'R. ESTABLISHED 1899.

c. 1910

The Old Hotel Washington in 1906. The Hill shown was 200 feet above the present street level, to realize the change see post card 3058.

c. 1906

Hotel Washington Annex

Seattle, Wash.

c. 1910

c. 1910

Hotel Washington, "The Scenic Hotel of the World," opened amid fanfare and six acres of landscaping in 1903. President Theodore Roosevelt was the first registered guest. In 1906, after a lavish farewell party, it was torn down so that Denny Hill could be sluiced into the bay.

42-STORY L. C. SMITH
BUILDING
The highest and finest and
best known office building
on the Pacific Coast.

Pierson Photo Co.

117662

c. 1930

Now dwarfed by a forest of office towers, the forty-two-story L. C. Smith Building was the tallest west of the Mississippi when it opened in 1914. The Chinese Room was the site of many high school graduation parties.

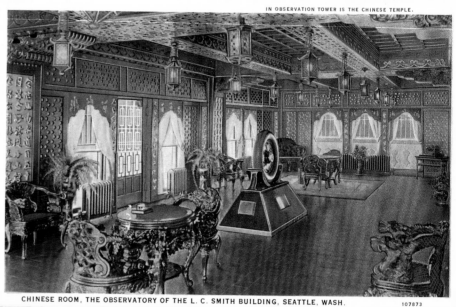

IN OBSERVATION TOWER IS THE CHINESE TEMPLE.

CHINESE ROOM, THE OBSERVATORY OF THE L. C. SMITH BUILDING, SEATTLE, WASH.   107873

c. 1930

THIS SPACE FOR WRITING MESSAGES

"C.T. ART-COLORTONE"

POST CARD
THIS SPACE FOR ADDRESS ONLY

UNITED STATES OF AMERICA
INDUSTRY AGRICULTURE

FOR DEFENSE

I'm writing this
from the Smith
Tower in Seattle.
Some airplanes came
over so low
that I thought they
were going to take
the Tower along.
Clarence

Mrs. Theo. Beck
522 E. Sumach
Walla Walla,
Wn.

c. 1945

c. 1910

Mount Rainier

as it looks on a clear day from Seattle, Fifty miles away, it is so brilliant and clear at times, that it seems but five.

c. 1950

c. 1940

c. 1940

c. 1945

1055 - FIRST HILL, SEATTLE, WASHINGTON, SHOWING THE CATHEDRAL.

c. 1910

Interior Catholic Cathedral, Seattle, Wash.

c. 1910

A corner of Madison Park, Seattle, Wash.

c. 1910

81 SEATTLE ART MUSEUM AND VOLUNTEER PARK

PHOTO BY ASAHEL CURTIS

5A-H884

c. 1945

1199 Shoot the Chutes Luna Park Seattle

c. 1905

3188 — Gunther's Observation Tree, Lake Burian, Seattle, Washington.

c. 1910

1201 The Natatorium Luna Park Seattle

c. 1905

Gunther's Observation Tree was the brainchild of a real estate developer. Prospects could pick their dream plat from atop the tower. Luna Park in West Seattle featured a saltwater swimming pool and the longest bar in town.

Seattle, Wash. Green Lake.
5576.

c. 1905

869 — LAKE WASHINGTON, DENNY-BLAINE PARK, SEATTLE, WASHINGTON
Come on in the water's great.
Maude
PUBLISHED BY E. P. CHARLTON & CO. SEATTLE, WASH.

c. 1905

2096
HAPPY DAYS, WOODLAND PARK, SEATTLE, WASH

c. 1910

THE BUFFALO HERD AT WOODLAND PARK, SEATTLE.

c. 1910

2770 – General View of Bellingham, Washington.

c. 1910

Commercial Avenue, Anacortes, Wash.

c. 1910

12227. Government Bulb Farm, Bellingham, Wash.

c. 1910

2766 – Scow Load of Salmon from the Traps, Bellingham, Washington.

c. 1910

West of the Mountains

For settlers in Western Washington, the first reality tended to be rain. Rain sluiced through the chinks in unfinished cabins. Rain turned the wagon roads to hopeless mud holes. Rain swelled the rivers, making crossings dangerous. Rain washed the starch out of the ladies' sunbonnets, leaving them flapping against their cheeks.

As generations of "wetsiders" have pointed out a bit defensively, it doesn't actually rain that much in most of Western Washington. It just seems that way. Drizzly autumns and winters are followed by showery springs, which often last well into July. After a couple of months when dust may actually become a problem, the rains return for the duration.

Nevertheless, like the Indians who came first, settlers found ample compensations. They might have mildew, but they lacked tornados, blizzards, droughts, and grasshopper plagues. Instead they found abundant seafood, plenty of timber, dazzling views, and dreams of glory.

By 1870, Western Washington was sprinkled with small communities, each sure that destiny was heading its way. From Whatcom to Vancouver, the woods hummed with boomers singing the praises of their chosen spots. All were in pursuit of what one of their number, the editor of the Quilcene *Megaphone*, called "the Roman god Terminus." Everyone knew that fortune followed the railroad into town.

In fact, fortune was just as likely to *precede* the railroad. Land in Union City, a hamlet on Hood Canal, sold for $1,000 an acre in

LAKE WHATCOM, BELLINGHAM, WASHINGTON.

c. 1910

anticipation of its namesake Union Pacific. The Panic of 1893 got there before the tracks did, however, and the UP went broke. A dozen other dream towns lived and died the same way.

After such disappointments the boomers generally left. The settlers settled in, turning their attention to the resources of the country. Bellingham built canneries and ran fish traps to support them. Everett and Tacoma specialized in lumber mills. Puyallup tried first hops, then flower bulbs. Port Blakely built ships. Allyn gathered oysters. Pending railroads and highways, towns got their goods to market via the ubiquitous Mosquito Fleet—steamers that plied the waters down Sound and upriver.

This world of small communities tucked in amidst the greenery was shattered by World War II. The Boeing Company's work force grew from four thousand in 1939 to fifty thousand in 1944, with corresponding jumps in the shipyards and military installations around the Sound. When peacetime came, many of these newcomers elected to stay. Suburbs began to sprout in farmers' fields. Holstein cattle made way for Boeing's expansion. By the 1980s, predictions of a megapolis extending from border to border along Interstate 5 seemed increasingly plausible. Four million people are expected around the Sound by the year 2020, nearly double the 1980 figure.

So far, though, much of the wetside has resisted homogenization. Many small towns still get by on the resources that won the loyalty of their founders. Lynden supplies the surrounding dairy farms. Elma depends on the vagaries of the timber industry. Bellingham still has fishing fleets and canneries, however diminished in size and profit.

Many descendents of the pioneer dreamers have a new goal, to bring their traditional trades into the twenty-first century. In the process they are helping to define the region's special magic.

City of Sumner.

c. 1910

Clark-Nickerson Lumber Mill, Everett, Wash.

c. 1910

Main Street, Mt. Vernon, Wash.

c. 1910

Birds Eye View, Snohomish, Wash.

c. 1910

Smelters, Irondale, Wash.

c. 1910

c. 1910

Daffodil fields of the Puyallup Valley with Mt. Rainier in the background

c. 1940

Daffodils serve double duty as a cash crop and a tourist attraction in the Puyallup and Skagit valleys. Each spring thousands of flowers are dyed improbable colors and worked into a float that carries the Daffodil Queen and Princesses through Tacoma, Puyallup, and Sumner.

c. 1910

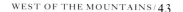

U. S. S. New York, Bremerton Navy Yard, Wash.

c. 1910

WISCONSIN

ATHLON

1223. See Battleships at Puget Sound Navy Yard. Ten round trips daily from Pier 2.

INLAND FLYER

c. 1910

Show this card to your Papa.

U. S. Submarine "Pike" showing Stern View, Puget Sound Navy Yard.

c. 1910

The Bremerton Navy Yard was contracted in 1892 and expanded during the Spanish American War. Its payroll and popularity grew with each conflict thereafter. "As far as the Pacific Coast is concerned, the sentiment is practically unanimous—in favor of our warlike enterprises in the South Seas," said *The Coast* magazine in February 1901.

Officers Quarters, Bremerton Navy Yard, Wash.

c. 1910

121 MOTOR FERRY "KALAKALA", WORLD'S FIRST STREAMLINED VESSEL

IN SERVICE BETWEEN SEATTLE AND BREMERTON, WASH. ON PUGET SOUND

5A-H1519

c. 1945

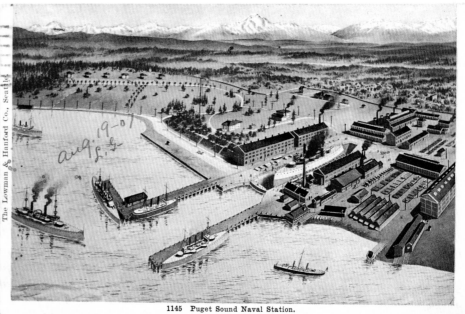

1145 Puget Sound Naval Station.

c. 1907

TACOMA, WASHINGTON,
GATEWAY TO RAINIER
NATIONAL PARK

c. 1910

New Tacoma Narrows Bridge is route to Olympic Peninsula vacationland.

c. 1945

Tacoma High School and Stadium,
4000 School Children forming a Flag.

Copyrighted 1910 By L. J. Brown.

c. 1910

A Glimse of the City Hall, Tacoma, Wash.

c. 1910

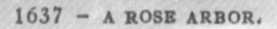

1637 – A ROSE ARBOR.

c. 1910

c. 1910

c. 1910

Mosquito Fleet ships swarmed into Commencement Bay for the dedication of the Eleventh Street Bridge in 1913. The *Verona* had one of the few female captains of the era, Gertrude Wiman. Under a different skipper, the *Verona* became notorious when members of the IWW chartered her for a trip that ended in the Everett Massacre of 1916.

Pacific Avenue, looking North from 13th Street, Tacoma, Wash.

c. 1910

PANTAGES THEATRE BUILDING, TACOMA, WASH.

c. 1905

Alexander Pantages entered show business in Alaska during the Gold Rush, then moved to Seattle in 1902. Twenty years later the illiterate Greek immigrant owned the biggest circuit in vaudeville. His Tacoma theater, built in 1916, has been renovated as a performing arts center.

View of Building of The Peoples Store Co. Tacoma, Wash.

12658

c. 1910

128. GEORGE LAWLER'S TULIP GARDEN, SHOWING 20,000 TULIPS IN BLOOM, GARDENVILLE, TACOMA, WASH.

c. 1925

THE COFFEE POT — ON PACIFIC HIGHWAY HALF-WAY BETWEEN TACOMA AND SO. TACOMA, WASH.

c. 1930

OLDEST CHURCH TOWER IN AMERICA, TACOMA, WASH.

c. 1925

St. Peter's Episcopal Church, Tacoma's first, was built in ten days in 1873. A charred stump served as bell tower, and children from a namesake church in Philadelphia donated a bell. Both church and stump are still in use.

c. 1910

Territorial government first met in 1853 in Olympia's only hotel. The capitol above was built in 1856, not 1852. Shortly after statehood, offices moved to the Thurston County Courthouse. Today's capitol was finished in 1928.

Washington State, named for the great
And as grand as her namesake is she.
Here's her building of state, her flower sedate,
And a greeting from me to thee.

c. 1908

c. 1940

c. 1917

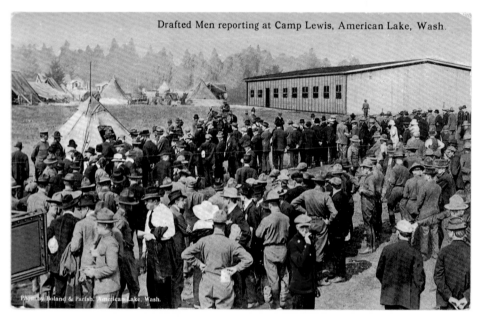

c. 1917

c. 1917

Inspired by patriotism and the vision of a permanent payroll, Pierce County citizens voted in 1917 to tax themselves two million dollars for a military base. Their gamble paid off. Tacoma mills got the biggest single lumber order in history and carpenters had Camp Lewis, now Fort Lewis, ready in time for World War I troops.

c. 1910

Centralia was founded by George Washington, a former slave who came to the territory in 1852 with his white adoptive parents. He platted his city in 1874, in time to profit from the arrival of the Northern Pacific railroad.

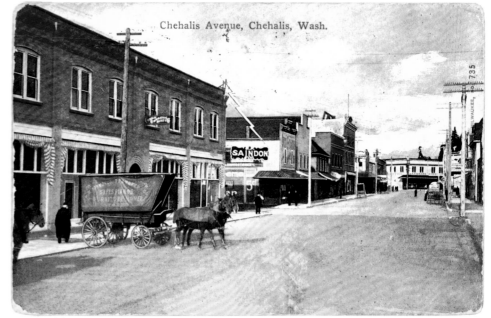

Chehalis Avenue, Chehalis, Wash.

c. 1910

POST CARD

LITHO-CHROME
TRADE MARK

Published by The Puget Sound News Company, Seattle, Wash.
Made in Germany
Dresden-Leipzig-Berlin
No. D3449

Postage
United States and
Island Possessions,
Cuba, Canada and
Mexico
ONE CENT.
For all other
Countries
TWO CENTS

Burlington June 26/12

Dear Mattie,-

All is well with me and business is fair. I hope you are feeling better all the time and that you managed to get your shoes changed for something you can wear. Mr. Hannaford's baby was born last Saturday morning at 8 months but both mother and babe are doing fine. Will

Mrs. Wm. A. Frost
4244 - 7th N.E.,
Seattle,
Wash.

c. 1912

Sectional View, Vancouver, Wash.

c. 1910

CATLIN WATERFRONT from KELSO, WASH.

c. 1910

713 INTERSTATE HIGHWAY BRIDGE, COLUMBIA RIVER, BETWEEN PORTLAND, OREGON AND VANCOUVER, WASH.

c. 1935

Main Street, looking North, Vancouver, Wash.

c. 1910

1625. Cascade Mountains, Wash., showing Cascade Pass at head of Stehekin River.

c. 1910

Mt. Agnes, Cascade Mountains, Washington.

c. 1910

692. Castle Rock, Lake Chelan, Wash.

Copyright by Curtis & Miller, Seattle, Wash.

c. 1910

July 28th 1907   No. 1318. Goat Hunting in Cascade Mountains, Washington

c. 1907

Cascades

The Cascades are among the world's most beautiful and most accessible mountain ranges. Visible from one hundred miles out on the Pacific, a confusion of rocky peaks runs from British Columbia to Northern California, topped at intervals by volcanic cones.

Indians generally stayed off the mountain slopes except for trade expeditions through Snoqualmie Pass. The occasional eruptions of Mount St. Helens were worked into their legends and passed on as warnings to the next generation.

Early European and American explorers used the mountains as a handy way to distribute favors, naming peaks for each other and for various stay-at-home dignitaries. Mount Baker—Koma Kulshan to the neighboring Nooksack Indians—now bears the name of the first Englishman to sight it. Mount Rainier honors a British admiral who never saw it.

However dull their nomenclature, the newcomers were moved by the mountains. In 1833, William Fraser Tolmie, a Hudson's Bay Company doctor, raved about "stupendous Rainier embosomed in cloud." Thomas Winthrop, a young writer, crossed the Cascades on horseback in 1853. By the end of the trip, he was convinced that so magnificent a landscape would help to create a new culture among those who lived there. For himself, he kept Rainier, as "an image of solemn beauty, which I could thenceforth evoke whenever in the world I must have peace or die."

For the more conventional, the Cascades were a giant, jumbled obstacle course. Settlers on both sides longed for a rail connection

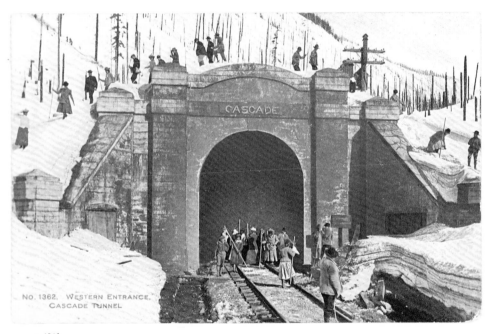

NO. 1362. WESTERN ENTRANCE, CASCADE TUNNEL

c. 1910

that would cross the Cascades and bypass Portland on the Columbia River. The first expedition in search of a railroad pass set forth in 1852, but Captain George McClellan (later to gain fame as a Civil War general), wasn't much interested. He and his crew walked past several passes, including Naches, where an immigrant party had crossed with 34 wagons and 171 people just weeks before. Still he saw no reason to alter his first impression of "mountain piled on mountain, rugged and impassable."

But McClellan's pessimism could only slow the inevitable. On May 3, 1888, drillers struck air after tunneling a railway route nearly two miles through Stampede Pass. In 1905, the first motorists braved the wagon road over Snoqualmie Pass, jacking up their flivvers to wrestle with rocks and stumps.

Roads meant visitors, an ever-growing army of Sunday drivers and weekend athletes. Residents of Cle Elum were the state's first skiers, taking to the slopes in the 1920s on homemade boards. Members of The Mountaineers, one of the first Northwest Alpine groups, began leading expeditions up Mount Rainier. Campaigns to preserve some of the finest views began almost as soon as anyone saw them.

While conservationists urged protection for their favorite spots, others put the mountains to work. Lumbermen and miners lobbied for roads. Rainier's image helped sell beer. Hydroelectric dams spanned some of the wildest of the Cascade rivers.

But the mountains are not tamed. In 1980, Mount St. Helens erupted again, killing at least sixty-nine people and devastating over one hundred fifty thousand acres of southwest Washington. The same spirit still stirs beneath other Cascade volcanoes, including Mount Baker and Glacier Peak. Even Rainier is not dead. Far below its glacial slopes lie pools of molten rock. When the earth shifts again, Rainier could become a mountain of fire.

"The Two Sentinels." Mt. Rainier, Washington.   1771

c. 1909

Mount Rainier, Washington. The Patriarch of the Cascades and one of the highest peaks in the American Continent.

c. 1910

Camping, Mt. Rainier, Wash.

c. 1910

Rainier National Park

138 Skiing on Mazama Ridge

8A-H123

c. 1940

MT. RAINIER AT SUNSET, NEAR OLYMPIA, WASHINGTON

© ASAHEL CURTIS

c. 1940

c. 1920

Bears were among the visitors when Paradise Lodge opened in 1917. They sometimes slept under the back stairs. Winter caretakers tunneled through hundred-foot snowdrifts to the building's second-story entrance.

c. 1923

c. 1920

P-1099 B-17 "Flying Fortress" over Mt Rainier, Wash.

c. 1950

198. Nature Coasting in Summer, Paradise Glacier
—— Rainier National Park ——

c. 1920

112. A Crevasse, Nisqually Glacier
Mt Rainier National Park, W⁹

c. 1920

Ice Cave in Paradise Glacier, Rainier National Park

c. 1920

c. 1910

c. 1910

c. 1945

Snoqualmie Falls was a popular excursion spot, accessible first by canoe, then by train from Seattle, and finally by car. By the teens, motorists would cross Snoqualmie Pass just to get some of Cora Chartrand's famous doughnuts.

c. 1910

Beautiful Washington — Mount St. Helens, Alt. 9,750 ft.

Beautiful Washington — Mount Adams

c. 1910

To woo voter support for expensive hydroelectric projects like Diablo Dam, Seattle City Light inaugurated two-day tours, with cruises on Diablo Lake, movies, and huge meals. Hot piped water warmed the soil for an exotic garden where orange trees grew amidst the Alpine firs, and the hills were alive with recorded bird songs.

Doubtful lake, — in the heart of the Cascades, Altitude 5050 ft. covers 160 acres, showing Glacier in Lake, also island — Spokane summer resort.

c. 1905

Tourist Steamer on Diablo Lake, Skaget, Washington

c. 1940

"See Washington First"
A crevasse on Roosevelt Glacier, Mt. Baker.

Photo by Sandison.

c. 1910

No. 1219   Steaming Crater of Mt. Baker.
COPYRIGHT BY B. & C. 1903

c. 1903

3008   MT. BAKER, WASH., BY MOONLIGHT FROM CHAIN LAKE

Photo by Sandison

c. 1910

Pack train ready to leave for Mt. Baker.

c. 1910

c. 1910

c. 1940

Spokane began as a couple of cabins beside an inadequate sawmill, overshadowed by towns like Colfax and Dayton. Prosperity came in the 1880s with the arrival of the railroads and the mining rush to the nearby Coeur d'Alene Mountains. Suddenly booming, the young city celebrated with substantial new buildings and bridges.

c. 1910

Inland Empire

Meandering downward from its source in the Canadian Rockies, the Columbia River links the wet and dry worlds of Washington. Its rapids and falls buried by the waters behind Grand Coulee Dam, it creeps through the Okanogan Highlands, where rounded hills overlook valley farms of irrigated fruit trees and alfalfa.

At the southern boundary of the highlands, the river swings west, then south and east through a desert landscape. Much of the Big Bend country has rainfall of less than ten inches a year. Tumbleweeds and dust devils chase each other across the drylands, and winter snows are blown into sinuous drifts.

Here, the grayish hills and bare, eroded rock have an austere beauty, and the soil needs only water and careful farming to be fertile. At Ginkgo Petrified Forest near Vantage, the remains of giant trees show what a different climate could produce. Ginkgos, oaks, maples, and sequoias thrived there ten million years ago, sheltering prehistoric camels, rhinoceros, and mastodon.

Shortly after joining the Snake River at Richland, the Columbia makes its final big turn west, heading for the Pacific. This is the Columbia Gorge, the ancient meeting grounds for the canoe Indians of the west side and the horse tribes of the Inland Empire. The Lewis and Clark Expedition followed the Gorge to the ocean, and immigrant parties of the Oregon Trail traveled by river en route to valleys beyond the Cascades.

At first, few people set out to settle the drylands. Some arrived exhausted at Walla Walla and decided to go no farther. Others saw

472— Western Approach to Spokane, Wash., over Sunset Highway #10

c. 1945

Dry Falls State Park, Washington

c. 1945

wheat-growing potential in the Palouse. Fur traders learned that livestock thrived on the bunchgrass of the Big Bend and the Okanogan. Many former trappers became ranchers.

Gold and silver strikes in the eastern Cascades, in the Okanogans, and in the Coeur d'Alenes across the Idaho border all brought swarms of newcomers, a few of whom prospered and some of whom stayed. As more settlements took hold in the 1850s, the Indians became increasingly uneasy. Yakimas, Spokanes, Pend Oreilles, and other tribes found themselves restricted from the fishing sites and grazing lands that provided their livelihood, and from the earth they revered as their mother. Even the reservations promised to them by treaty were not secure. Under pressure from settlers and miners, the government failed to enforce their boundaries. The Indian wars that followed were protracted and heartbreaking. When they were over, the Inland Empire was available for the pursuit of American dreams.

One of the dreamers was James N. Glover, a successful merchant in the Willamette Valley who wanted to found a town of his own. He located his ideal spot in 1873 at Spokane Falls. Few gamblers would have bet on the settlement's prospects as a regional metropolis. Walla Walla, for example, had nearly a twenty-year head start and a strong agricultural base. But Glover was persistent and eventually fortune smiled. The silver strike at Kellog, Idaho, was a goldmine for Spokane, which built hotels, banks, suppliers, saloons, and other accoutrements of mining life. The Spokane River flowed nearly unseen beneath the railway bridges, and the first hydroelectric plant west of the Mississippi lit the streets at night and ran streetcars in the daytime.

By 1900, Glover's collection of cabins had become a city of over a hundred thousand people. For the isolated ranchers and miners, Spokane was truly the bright lights, the big city.

320. C. M. & St. P. Train Crossing Spokane River, Spokane, Wash.

c. 1910

80. Lower Falls, Spokane, Wash.

c. 1910

485 – LOWER FALLS, SPOKANE, WASHINGTON.

c. 1910

Early settlers found Spokane Falls beautiful but unpromising. The area had gravelly soil, little rain, and no roads. James N. Glover saw the falls and fell in love. He made them the centerpiece of the city he platted in 1878.

432. Main Avenue, Spokane, Wash.

c. 1915

ONE OF DURKIN'S SALOONS IN SPOKANE
A Baptist Minister decorated the windows of this house.

c. 1910

HYDROPATHIC SANITARIUM
204 WEST INDIANA AVE.
SPOKANE, WASHINGTON.

c. 1910

293. CENTRAL FIRE DEPARTMENT, SPOKANE, WASH.
UP TO DATE AUTO EQUIPMENT.

c. 1910

c. 1910

Gonzaga College Drill, Spokane, Wash.

c. 1910

c. 1910

Once the Great Northern Railway joined Spokane to Seattle in 1892, wheat from the Inland Empire could go straight from Jim Hill's railroad to Jim Hill's steamships to markets in Asia. Back in town, the marketing efforts of Washington Water Power brought streetlights and electric trolleys to nearly every corner.

c. 1910

c. 1910

c. 1920

Flamboyant hotelier Louis Davenport opened his hostelry in 1914 and it was Spokane's best for sixty years. The poet Vachel Lindsay lived there from 1924 to 1929, his rent subsidized by the hotel as a public relations expense.

c. 1910

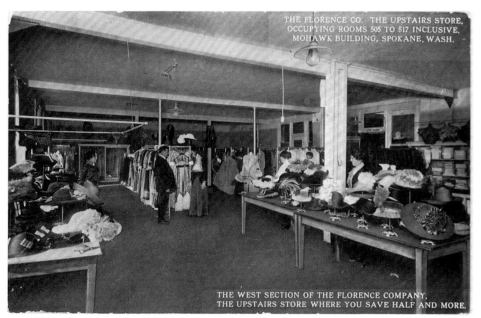

THE FLORENCE CO. THE UPSTAIRS STORE, OCCUPYING ROOMS 505 TO 517 INCLUSIVE, MOHAWK BUILDING, SPOKANE, WASH.

THE WEST SECTION OF THE FLORENCE COMPANY, THE UPSTAIRS STORE WHERE YOU SAVE HALF AND MORE.

c. 1910

HOTEL MAJESTIC
SPOKANE, WASH.

Hotel Majestic,
Strictly Modern
Rates $1.00 and up
324 First Avenue,
Spokane, Wash.

c. 1910

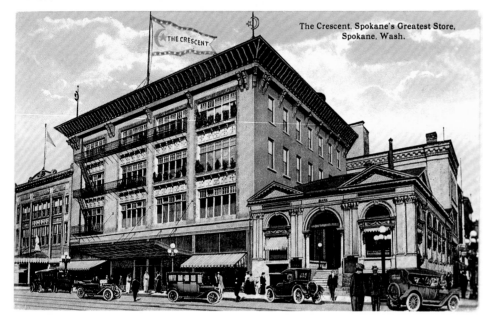

THE CRESCENT

The Crescent, Spokane's Greatest Store, Spokane, Wash.

c. 1910

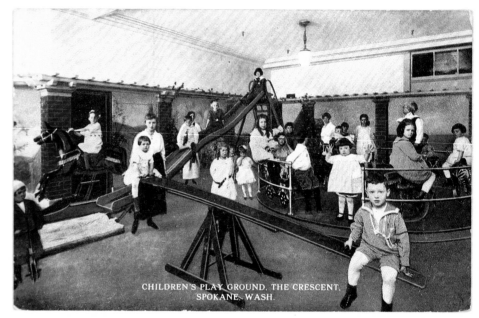

CHILDREN'S PLAY GROUND, THE CRESCENT, SPOKANE, WASH.

c. 1910

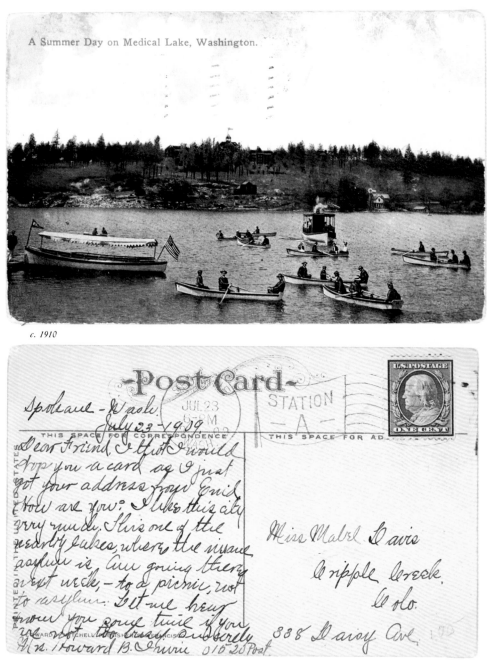

A Summer Day on Medical Lake, Washington.

c. 1910

c. 1909

1469:—Down River Municipal Golf Course from Club House, Spokane, Wash.

c. 1925

Medical Lake's soothing, soda-rich waters were first used by neighboring Indians. The lake was developed as a resort by Washington Water Power, which ran an electric train out from Spokane. Another electric railway served Manito Park, just south of downtown.

Southeast Boulevard, Spokane, Wash.

c. 1910

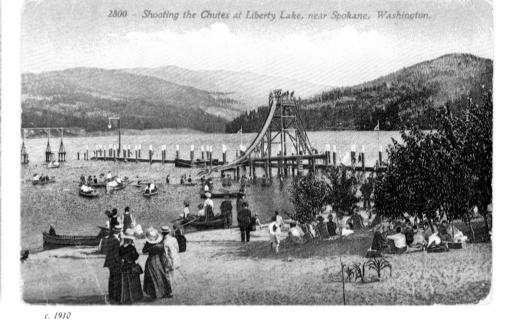

2800 – Shooting the Chutes at Liberty Lake, near Spokane, Washington.

c. 1910

One of Spokane's Many Beautiful Camping Resorts

c. 1910

1116 – NEWMAN LAKE, NEAR SPOKANE, WASHINGTON.

c. 1910

190. SPOKANE INDIAN.

c. 1910

Yakima Squaw and Papoose

c. 1910

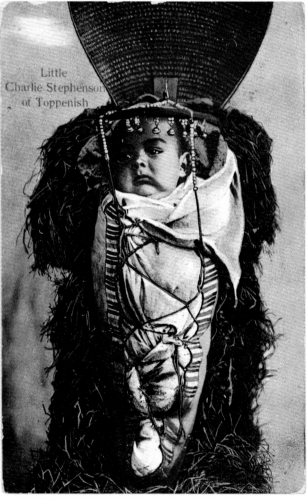

Little Charlie Stephenson of Toppenish

c. 1910

More than the coastal tribes, the Yakimas, Spokanes, Nez Perce, and other inland groups satisfied white stereotypes of what Indians should look like. Families could earn a little money by posing for postcards and snapshots.

1538. Indian Agency in the Northwest.
Nespelem, Wash.

c. 1910

1539. Indian Camp on the Colville Reservation,
Washington.

c. 1910

Block House. Fort Simcoe.   Yakima Indian Reservation.

c. 1910

275-CALISPELL INDIANS AT SI-SI-AH CREEK,
PEND OREILLE RIVER, WASH.

c. 1910

Photo by Asahel Curtis.   "See Washington First."   The Olympian in Kittitas Valley.
On the Line of the C. M. & P. S. R. R.

c. 1910

THE ORIENTAL LIMITED
Chicago, St. Paul, Minneapolis, Spokane, Seattle, Tacoma and North Pacific Coast Points

Kept free from dirt and dust with Vacuum cleaning machines.
Other distinctive features are: Daily News Bulletin. Telephone
Connections and Afternoon Tea Service in the Observation Car.
Electric Lighted Throughout.   Compartment Observation Cars.
THE PERFECT TRAIN TO PUGET SOUND

c. 1910

Depot, Inland Empire Railway System,
Garfield, Wash.

c. 1910

The first trains in the Inland Empire went thirty-one miles
from Walla Walla to the river port of Wallula. The wooded
rails were surfaced with rawhide, which proved irresistible
to coyotes and had to be replaced with iron.

From Sage Brush to Harvest, Washington.

c. 1910

HARVEST FIELD. WASHINGTON.

c. 1910

Ritzville Flouring Mill, Ritzville, Wash.

RITZVILLE FLOURING MILL

MILL OFFICE

c. 1910

Overflow of Wheat.

c. 1910

Old Mill, Republic, Wash.   Pub. by The New York Bazaar, Republic, Wash.

c. 1910

A Washington Cattle Scene.

c. 1910

Kennewick, Washington, in 1899.

c. 1910

In a bad winter, a warm Chinook wind could uncover enough grass to salvage starving livestock. Ranchers endorsed the prayer published in 1872 by The *Weekly Mountaineer* in The Dalles, Oregon: "O Stockman's God! O Thou/To whom we always look/And humbly, trusting bow/In prayer and praise—CHINOOK!"

Mt. Adams from Sunnyside Canal, Yakima Valley, Washington.

"A Busy Day in North Yakima, Wash."

c. 1910

North Coast Gasoline Motor Car, North Yakima, Wash.

c. 1910

1716. Chimney Rocks on Atanum Road, near North Yakima, Wash.

c. 1910

A series of lava flows some twenty million years ago covered a quarter-million miles of the Columbia Plateau with basalt, and set the stage for amazing formations, including the striped curves of the channeled scablands and these chimney rocks, exposed by erosion from the Yakima River.

c. 1910

A Rare Scene of the Court House at Walla Walla, Wash.

c. 1910

1614. Main Street, Walla Walla, Wash.

c. 1910

Walla Walla was a supply center for the Idaho goldfields in the 1860s, making it the largest community in Washington Territory. After the gold was gone, the town found its treasure in the nearby wheat farms of the Palouse. This prosperous past has left a legacy of gracious streets and notable nineteenth-century architecture.

Walla Walla Oct 30.
Dear Fransis
    I tank you for the nise little card I got from you. Mama is a strike now, she dont write. so now you Chuldne will have two. How do you like this Card, Walla Walla in Winter. you probaly tink that W.W. has not got eny Winter. but we have, lots of Snow and cold. at present it is rather cold and raw. and I feel it very mutch Papa

POST CARD
This side for address

WALLA WALLA
OCT 31 5 30 PM 1912 WASH.

11224—SHROUSE & SON, TACOMA, WASH., PUBLISHERS.

Miss Frances Berger
1145 Fanguni St
St Paul
Minn.

c. 1912

Palouse River Washington.

c. 1910

Steptoe Butte, Washington.

c. 1910

Sixth St. Clarkston, Wash.

c. 1910

THIS SPACE FOR WRITING MESSAGES.

POST CARD

c. 1909

c. 1910

Sometimes big game was in the eye of the beholder. In Seattle in 1900, a circus reject was released in Leschi Park so Sarah Bernhardt could shoot a bear in the wilderness. The French actress took the skin home to Paris.

c. 1910

c. 1910

Saddle Rock, Wenatchee, Wash.

c. 1910

Overlooking apple orchards along the Columbia River in Washington State's Wenatchee Valley

c. 1945

An Irrigated Orchard, Washington.

c. 1910

268. Cashmere, Wenatchee Valley, Wash.

c. 1910

MANY PASSENGER STEAMERS PLY UP AND DOWN THIS GREAT STREAM.

233. TOURIST TRIP ON THE BEAUTIFUL COLUMBIA.

c. 1920

700. Vantage Ferry on Columbia River, Washington.

104479

c. 1910

CONTROL BOARDS IN POWERHOUSE AT GRAND COULEE DAM, WASHINGTON—210

c. 1950

Grand Coulee Dam in State of Washington, man's greatest engineering project

c. 1950

"See Washington First." Looking down the Columbia River near White Salmon on the North Bank Road.

Photo by C. C. Hutchins.

c. 1910

GREAT KETTLE FALLS OF THE COLUMBIA, EASTERN WASHINGTON.

c. 1910

Cape Horn, Banks of the Columbia River.

c. 1910

The Lewis and Clark Expedition made camp near Cape Horn on the trip west. The explorers built extra fires that night to dry bedding and kill fleas. Upriver, the fishing grounds at Kettle Falls are lost behind Grand Coulee Dam.

Harvesting Large Acreages of Wheat in Washington, with combined Harvester and Thresher

c. 1910

Thrashing Oats in Whatcom County

c. 1910

№ 1425. A Washington Cornfield.

c. 1910

Breaking Virgin Soil, Washington.

c. 1910

Farm and Forest

Land, free at first and cheap later, was the lure that brought people west. Farmers wanted fertile acres. Loggers wanted endless timber. Postcards promised it all.

Tired of your patch of Vermont gravel? Come to Washington and grow cabbages the size of washtubs and corn like cordwood. Even the mammoth trees were used to promote farming, on the theory that soil that produced them could grow anything.

This was not true, as many stump farmers learned to their sorrow. The trees were tenacious, and the soil beneath them thin. The stumps themselves could serve as shelter in a pinch though. Unlike big corn, stump houses were not just a photographer's joke. They did serve as temporary homes for people or livestock.

Trees were Washington's most obvious asset. Especially west of the Cascades, the hillsides of dark conifers variegated with alders and flaming vine maple turned men's thoughts to trade. Seattle's first sale was a load of pilings for San Francisco. Its first business was a sawmill. A mill meant boards for real clapboard houses, no more log cabins. It meant docks and boardwalks. It meant mill hands with paychecks to spend. Still, logs and a place to slice them did not guarantee prosperity. Washington was far from major markets, and transport by schooner was expensive and slow.

The tide turned in 1900 when Frederick Weyerhaeuser bought nine hundred thousand acres of Northwest timber, and James J. Hill provided the railway to ship the harvest east. The forests of the Great Lakes were about played out, and lumbermen and

2820 - Grain Fields in the Foothills of the West, near Spokane, Washington.

c. 1910

loggers headed to Washington. Soon Weyerhaeuser became the world's biggest timber company and Washington the major timber state. And it was not much longer before overcutting threatened the future of mill towns throughout the region.

Agriculture followed a similar cycle. Early homesteads were necessarily self-sufficient, generally including a milk cow, a laying flock, draft animals, vegetables, and grain. Not knowing what to expect from the soil or the climate in their new home, settlers tried a bit of everything.

Challenges varied with the territory. East of the Cascades the volcanic soil was generally fertile but water was scarce. Bad winters could decimate a rancher's promising herd, and dust storms and grasshoppers blighted many a farmer's hopes. To the west the climate was moist and mild but the soil, often the gravelly souvenir of an Ice Age glacier, was unthrifty. The richest land lay in the river valleys. Farmers in the soggy Skagit Flats outfitted their horses with special mud-walking shoes the size of serving plates. Thus equipped they raised bumper crops of cabbages, peas, and hay in the diked delta.

Eventually specialization set in. Dairies, truck farms, flowers, and berries are concentrated west of the mountains, near the big cities that provide their markets. The Inland Empire looks outside the region for its customers, shipping wheat, fruits, potatoes, and livestock. Automated irrigation and giant combines have turned thousand-acre wheat farms into one-man operations, while the orchards of the Wenatchee and Yakima valleys still depend on an annual infusion of migrant labor.

Though wheat brings in more revenue, the apple has become the icon of Washington agriculture. Polished to a mirror shine from its glossy shoulders to its five-pointed base, the Red Delicious is the state's best-known ambassador.

The Berry Pickers.

c. 1910

c. 1910

c. 1910

The volcanic soil of the Yakima Valley is fertile but dry, with rainfall averaging under ten inches a year. The first irrigation project in the valley, about 1850, was a collaboration between Kamiakin, a Yakima tribal leader, and the priests at St. Joseph's Catholic mission.

c. 1910

c. 1910

c. 1910

c. 1910

Bountiful harvests meant heavy work for pickers and pruners, including Bill Douglas, a Yakima boy who became Chief Justice of the U.S. Supreme Court. On the proudest day of his childhood he picked 400 pounds of cherries.

Picking Apples in the Famous Fruit Growing Kittitas Valley, Washington, near Ellensburg
GEO. B. HAYNES, Gen. Pass. Agt., C. M. & St. P. Ry., Chicago; GEO. W. HIBBARD, Gen. Pass. Agt., Seattle, Wash.
O. E. SHANER, Immigration Agt., Chicago; J. H. GINET, JR., Immigration Agt., Seattle, Wash.

c. 1910

c. 1940

c. 1910

The prototypical Washington apple is the Delicious—huge, glossy, and photogenic. Its picturebook appearance has given it preeminence over more flavorful varieties.

c. 1910

c. 1910

Indians worked the hop harvest, bringing specially made baskets to hold the papery cones. In the 1880s, North Bend claimed the world's largest hop farm.

c. 1910

Digging Potatoes in Washington.

c. 1907

Mammoth Vegetables, Washington.

COPYRIGHT 1908
BY M.L.OAKES.

c. 1908

Non-Irrigated Farm in Suburbs of Spokane, Wash.

c. 1909

Loading Mammoth
Washington Corn.

c. 1909

Shearing Sheep, Washington.

c. 1910

2127 – Dairy Herd at the Stream, near Spokane, Washington.

c. 1910

3060. Cowboys rounding up Range Cattle, in the Northwest.

c. 1910

The Hudson's Bay Company established the first ranches in Washington, hiring Indians as cowboys. Chief Factor John McLoughlin loaned breeding animals to settlers to get their own herds started. Before long, stockmen and farmers were skirmishing over grazing rights and fences.

c. 1910

Two Natives of Washington.
A Bear Den and Dwelling in a Washington
Saw Log.

c. 1910

2100 Leisure Hour in a Western Logging Camp.

c. 1910

Cradle for Ocean-Going Log Raft, Puget Sound, Washington.

c. 1910

Washington "Tooth Picks."

c. 1910

A Washington Forest Home

c. 1905

Yellow Pine Tooth Picks, Washington

c. 1910

LOGGING IN WASHINGTON.

c. 1905

Early commercial logging was done at the water's edge. Trees were simply rolled into the water. Later came the ox team and the skid road, whose notched logs were greased with dogfish oil to reduce friction.

Class of School Children on single Cedar Stump, Washington.

c. 1910

c. 1910

c. 1910

Photographers loved to pose their subjects atop, alongside, or inside giant timber. The home-in-a-stump theme was so popular that a postcard of one Snohomish County residence was simply relabeled for sale as a souvenir of Oregon.

283. The Panhandle Lumber Mill at Ione, Wash.
Twenty hour capacity 250,000 feet.

c. 1910

Dumping Logs from train into river, Washington

c. 1910

Log Jam on the Spokane River, Washington.

c. 1910

BIG TREES OF THE PACIFIC COAST — A LOGGING TRAIN.

c. 1910

c. 1912

c. 1910

The Tourist Hotel was still incomplete when it burned in 1896. It was resurrected ten years later as Tacoma High School, and became a civic symbol. Boosters boasted that "they are even printing postcards of it in Germany."

c. 1950

Celebrations

Indians held the first celebrations in what is now called Washington. They honored the salmon that sustained them with a ceremony at the start of each fishing season. Potlatches and winter dances drew communities together to mark important events and to pass on religious traditions.

The whites brought their own rituals. For Americans, the Fourth of July was always good for a party. The first official Fourth west of the Rockies was the inspiration of Lieutenant Charles Wilkes, the otherwise unpopular captain of the United States Exploring Expedition. Held in 1841, it followed a format which soon became familiar.

A young bull was roasted over alder coals. Sailers played ball, and, lacking women, danced with each other. Speakers prophesied prosperity. A howitzer misfired and mangled a sailor's hand. Similar events took place wherever Americans congregated. Sometimes they tended toward delinquency. In the 1850s, oyster dealers on Shoalwater Bay set stumps on fire, touching off a blaze that burned out of control until the fall rains.

Later, communities organized more decorous observances. Most towns had a harvest fair, and these eventually consolidated into county and regional events. The Puyallup Fair, begun in the 1890s with "a bull and a goose," now dominates the genre. Each September it offers everything from 4-H rabbit judging to big-name bands.

William O. Douglas, later Chief Justice of the U.S. Supreme Court, grew up with the Yakima County Fair, working as a ticket

c. 1912

c. 1909

taker for the Educated Horse and The Tunnel of Love. Elsewhere on the grounds men competed in the matters of richest alfalfa and most prolific sow, while their wives faced off with needlework, flowers, and pies. Around the state, nearly every flower still receives its due, with Daffodil Festivals in the Puyallup Valley, Apple Blossom Festivals in Wenatchee, Lilac Festivals in Spokane and Tulip Festivals in the Skagit.

Unwilling to surrender entirely to the melting pot, communities celebrate their ethnic heritage with parties like Deutches Fest in Odessa, Bon Odori and Festival Sundiata in Seattle, and Makah Days at Neah Bay. Other events elevate workaday jobs into performances. Loggers in Deming compete at log rolling and spar climbing. Farmers groom their draft horses and plow specimen furrows in Monroe and Lynden. Cowboys rope calves and ride bulls in Ellensburg and Omak.

County fairs offer continuity, the soothing knowledge that our children's children will find the same cotton candy and flop-eared rabbits we did. Big-city extravaganzas may leave more than memories. In addition to acres of temporary plaster, the Alaska-Yukon-Pacific Exposition, held at the University of Washington in 1909, created campus landmarks such as Frosh Pond and Rainier Vista. The massive Forestry Building, "the largest log cabin in the world," does not survive. It was found to house possibly the world's largest collection of wood-eating beetles.

The Century 21 Exposition, the state's first World Fair, left Seattle the Space Needle, the Monorail, and the Pacific Science Center. In Spokane, Expo '74 brought international attention, a new opera house, and River Front Park.

Whether they arise from sheer civic enthusiasm or more commercial concerns, celebrations serve one common function. More than any other event, they let us see how a town sees itself.

X77 Agricultural, European and Alaska Building.

Official Post Card.

c. 1909

THE IMMENSE ARENA OF "THE BATTLE OF THE MONITOR AND MERRIMAC." A GREAT MARINE BATTLE SPECTACLE COSTING $240,000.   LOCATED ON THE PAY STREAK, ALASKA-YUKON-PACIFIC EXPOSITION, SEATTLE, WASH., U. S. A.

Copyright 1909
by E. W McConnell
Riverview Park, Chicago

c. 1909

X106 Collonade of Forestry Building.

Official Post Card.

c. 1909

ESKIMO TRIBES OF SIBERIA AND ALASKA, ALASKA, YUKON, PACIFIC EXPOSITION, 1909
(OFFICIAL POST CARD.)   SEATTLE, WASH.

c. 1909

c. 1908

AYP designers were fond of barebreasted allegory. The grounds were crowded with paintings and plaster statues featuring maidens in consort with salmon, electric wires, and other icons of the region's economy.

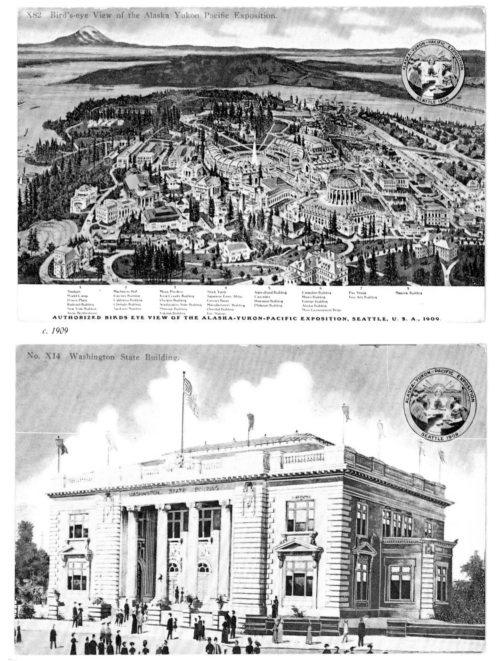

c. 1909

c. 1909

c. 1962

c. 1962

c. 1962

Fifty years after AYP, Seattle felt ready to play host to the world. The Century 21 Exposition in 1961 gave the city its best-known building, the Space Needle. A commemorative pasta, the Space Noodle, did not catch on.

c. 1913

The National Apple Show spotlighted the changing fashions in pomoculture. The Spitzbergens and Grimes Goldens of 1910 were orchard heirlooms by the 1950s.

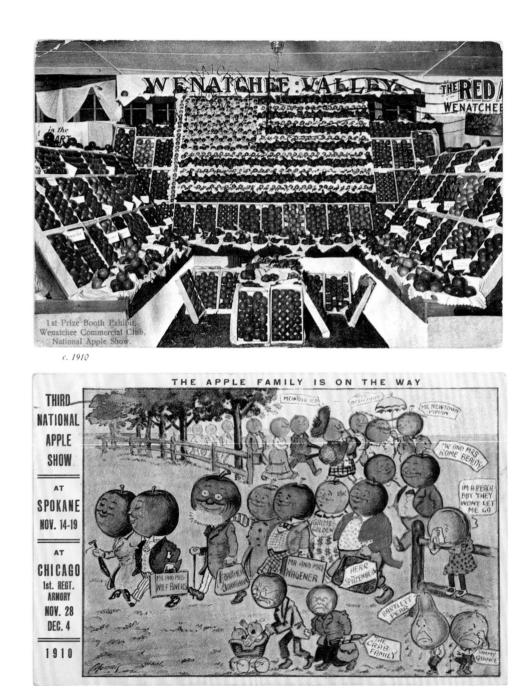

c. 1910

c. 1910

Fair Hesperides—North Central Washington Exposition, Wenatchee, Wash., Oct. 26th to 31st, 1914.

c. 1914

c. 1913

Nearly every community had its annual festival and parade. Walla Walla celebrated the sowing of winter wheat. Wenatchee honored the goddess of apples, and Spokane rolled out a thirty-two-foot potato.

Our Great Big Baked Potato Float, Exhibited in E-Nak-ops Jubilee Parade, Spokane, Wash. Size of Potato 32 feet long, 16 feet wide, 14 feet high.

c. 1910

c. 1913

c. 1913

c. 1913

c. 1913

c. 1910

Saengerfest
Walla Walla, Wash.
June 19-23, 1913.

c. 1913

Nearly every community had its annual festival and parade. Walla Walla celebrated the sowing of winter wheat. Wenatchee honored the goddess of apples, and Spokane rolled out a thirty-two-foot potato.

c. 1913

c. 1913

c. 1913

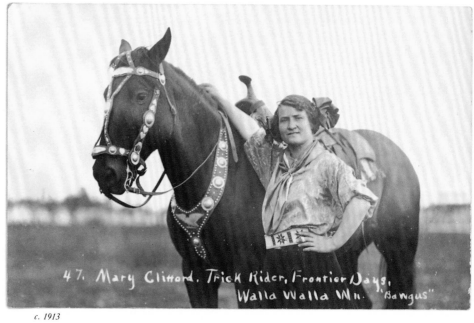

c. 1913

Float in Industrial Parade, Golden Potlatch, Seattle, Washington.

c. 1912

Decorated Automobile, Golden Potlatch Parade, Seattle, Washington.

c. 1912

Decorated Auto, Golden Potlatch Parade, Seattle, Washington.

c. 1912

In 1911, the first Golden Potlatch was billed as "six days of innocent amusement," with parades on land and water. The short-lived festival traded on associations with the Gold Rush and traditional Indian observances, hence the name.

c. 1940

Acknowledgements

I would like to thank Carla St. John, Charles Payton, Paul Dorpat, Carolyn Marr, and my father, Murray Morgan, for their help with research questions, and my husband and daughter, Bruce and Laurel Brown, for their patience.